Good Luck

Create the Conditions for Success in Life and Business

Alex Rovira

Fernando Trías de Bes

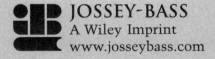

JOSSEY-BASS
A Wiley Imprint
www.josseybass.com

Published by Jossey-Bass
A Wiley Imprint
989 Market Street, San Francisco, CA 94103-1741
www.josseybass.com

Illustrations © Josep Feliu, 2004.

Jossey-Bass books and products are available through most bookstores.
To contact Jossey-Bass directly call our Customer Care Department
within the U.S. at 800-956-7739, outside the U.S. at 317-572-3986, or
fax 317-572-4002.

Jossey-Bass also publishes its books in a variety of electronic formats.
Some content that appears in print may not be available in electronic
books.

Library of Congress Cataloging-in-Publication Data

Rovira, Alex.
    Good luck : create the conditions for success in life and business /
Alex Rovira, Fernando Trías de Bes.
        p. cm.
        ISBN 0-7879-7607-5 (alk. paper)
    1. Success.   2. Success in business.   3. Fortune.   I. Trías de Bes,
Fernando.   II. Title.
        BF637.S8R64 2004
        158.1—dc22   2004012067

Printed in the United States of America
FIRST EDITION
HB Printing   10 9 8 7 6 5 4 3 2 1

Contents

For my children, Laia and Pol,
and for all the children for whom stories are written.
Also for the child we all have inside no matter our age,
as this is the one with the joy, longing, and passion
for life, necessary ingredients for Good Luck.

For my parents, Gabriel and Carmen,
for their love, faith, and example. And for all
the parents whose love for their children
becomes the seed of Good Luck.

To my mate, Mónica,
and to all human beings who devote their lives
to others as they are the living proof that stories,
as well as life, can have a happy ending.

Alex Rovira

For Guillermo Trías de Bes, my father,
with all my love and gratitude, since he is
the one who taught me the rules of Good Luck,
not with a fable, but by his example.
Indeed, my father is the main reason
I know Good Luck can be created.
He showed me that, basically, it's all about
faith, generosity, and Love, in caps.

Fernando Trías de Bes

Part One

The Encounter

One fine afternoon in spring, Max, a prosperous and discreet businessman, elegantly yet casually dressed, sat on his favorite bench in Central Park and watched couples strolling by, children playing, and trees swaying in the gentle breeze. He was thinking about his life. His bare feet rested in the clover-strewn grass; everything was just as he liked it to be these afternoons he spent in Central Park.

Max was sixty-four years old and had had a life full of success.

All of a sudden, something unexpected happened.

Another man, also sixty-four, sat down beside him: Jim. Jim looked like a beaten man, a tired man, but a man who, nevertheless, managed still to walk with dignity. Jim was going through some hard times. In fact, his life had been rough for the last fifty years. Things had not been going well for him for a very long time.

When Jim sat down next to Max, they looked at each other. Each recognized in the other's eyes something familiar . . . very distant but very familiar.

"Max?" asked Jim.

"Jim?" answered Max.

"No!" cried Jim.

"I can't believe it!" shouted Max.

They stood up and laughed and gave each other a big hug.

Max and Jim had been very close friends in their early childhood, from the time they were two years old until the day they turned ten. They had been neighbors in the Bronx, the humble neighborhood in New York where they had spent their early years.

"I recognized your unique blue eyes," Max told Jim.

"And I recognized your straightforward and sincere look . . . the one you had . . . fifty-four years ago . . . and hasn't changed a bit," answered Jim.

After remembering and sharing some childhood memories, Max said to Jim:

"My old friend, tell me how you've been. I can see in your eyes a bit of sadness."

Jim answered:

"My life has been a sum of failures."

"Why?" asked Max.

"As you probably remember, we left the neighborhood when I was about ten. We just moved out one day, never to return. The reason was an immense fortune that my father inherited from an uncle who had no descendants. We left without saying a word. My parents didn't want people to know about this unexpected turn of events. We changed our home, our car, our neighbors, our friends. That day you and I lost contact."

"So that's what happened," said Max. "We always wondered what happened to you. So this fortune was so enormous?"

"Yes. And a great part of what we inherited was a very profitable, huge textile factory in full operation. My father made it still bigger and more profitable. When he died, I took control of it. But I had very bad luck. Everything went wrong," explained Jim.

"So, what exactly happened?" asked Max.

"For quite some time I made no changes, since things seemed to be going fine. But then competitors started to emerge everywhere and sales began to drop off. Our product was the best there was so I was hoping our customers would see that our competitors' product, though cheaper, was inferior. But our customers knew nothing about cloth or fabrics. If they had, they would have understood that our product was better. But they kept choosing the products of the newer, trendier companies."

Jim took a deep breath. Remembering all that was not easy. Max kept quiet. He didn't know what to say. Jim continued:

"I lost a lot of money but the business was still in operation. I tried to simplify things and reduce the size of the business, cut costs as much as I could, but the smaller we got, the lower the sales went. We considered creating a new brand but couldn't find the backers to invest in it. The market wanted foreign brands. That didn't leave me too many options. I thought about opening a chain of my own stores and researched it for almost a year. When we finally did, I wasn't able to cover the cost of the stores—sales just weren't high enough. I started to default on my loan payments. So I had to sell the factory, the land, my house, all my property. I had everything, all I ever wanted, and I lost it all. Luck was never on my side."

"What did you do then?" asked Max.

"Nothing. I didn't know what to do. All the people who had been on my side were now walking away. Even my wife left me. I'd ruined that relationship too. I went from one job to the next, but couldn't fit in. It reached a point where I even knew what hunger was. For the last fifteen years I have been trying to survive the best I can, making a living off the tips I get for running errands and even accepting a little help from the folks in my neighborhood. Life hasn't brought me very much luck."

Jim didn't feel like going on so he asked his childhood friend:

"And what about you? What of your life? Have you had any luck?"

Max smiled.

"As you will remember, my parents were poor, even poorer than yours when you were in the neighborhood. My origins are more than humble, you know that well: they were precarious. Many nights we had nothing to eat. Do you remember that even your mother brought us food sometimes because she knew how hard things were for us at home? I think you also know I wasn't able to go to school, I just studied in the so-called College of Life. I started working when I was ten, just after you and your family disappeared so mysteriously."

Max continued:

"I started washing cars. Then I got a job in a luxury hotel as a bellboy. Later I got promoted and worked as a doorman at several luxury hotels. When I was twenty-two, I took a big chance."

"What did you do?" asked Jim with some curiosity.

"I bought a small workshop that was about to close. I bought it with a loan and all the savings I had at the time. It was a workshop that made leather bags. I had seen all kinds of bags at the restaurants and fancy hotels were I'd worked. So I knew what the rich liked. I just had to make what I had carried so many times in my hands as a bellboy."

Max went on:

"At first, I had to make the bags and sell them at the same time. I worked nights and weekends. The first year was very good, and I invested everything I made in more raw material and traveled all over the country to find out what other people were doing. I had to know more than anyone else about leather bags. I learned a lot visiting stores. I asked anyone I saw with a leather bag what it was that they liked or disliked about their bag."

Max remembered with passion those first years. He continued:

"Sales started to go up. For ten years I reinvested everything I made. I looked for new opportunities where I thought they could be found. Each year I modified the bags that sold best, always improving their design. I never left a problem at the workshop unsolved for the next day. I tried to be in charge of whatever happened around me. I acquired a second workshop, and then another one, and another one. . . . Finally, now I have over two thousand employees in twenty factories around the world. Truth is, it was worth it, but it wasn't easy, it was a lot of work."

Jim interrupted him at this point, wanting to comment on that last statement:

"See, you had more luck than me. That's all."

"You think so? You really think I was just lucky?" exclaimed Max, surprised.

"I don't mean to be annoying or to belittle you," Jim answered in a thin voice. "But don't think you are the cause of your success. Fortune smiles on those whom destiny cares to choose. It smiled at you and not at me. That's all, my old friend."

Max was thoughtful for a while. After some time he said:

"Listen, I didn't inherit any great fortune, but I inherited something that is much better, thanks to my grandfather. Do you know the difference between luck and Good Luck, with capital letters?"

"No, I don't," Jim replied, showing little interest.

"I learned the difference between luck and Good Luck from a story my grandfather used to tell me when he was living with us. Many times I thought, and still do, that this legend changed my life. It has been with me in times of fear, doubt, uncertainty, and confusion, and also at times of happiness and gratitude. Thanks to this story I decided to buy that old workshop with the money that had taken me six years to save. This story helped me make a lot of other decisions, too, that later proved to be crucial in my life."

Max kept talking, while Jim remained with his gaze lost elsewhere.

"Perhaps, at sixty-four one is not in the mood to hear stories but it is never too late to hear something that might be useful. As they say, 'while there's life, there's hope.' If you want, I can tell you the story."

Jim didn't answer.

"This story has helped a lot of people. Not just businessmen—entrepreneurs, and men and women of all crafts and skills. People who learned the

difference between luck and Good Luck have
achieved spectacular results at their jobs and great
results for the companies for which they work. It's
helped others find their mates, helped them find that
person they always dreamed of, to care for and
deepen that love. This story has been helpful to
athletes, entertainers, even to scientists and
researchers, people of all ages. And I can tell you this
because I have seen it firsthand; I'm sixty-four and
have seen the effect of this legend on many people."

Jim said:

"All right, tell me: what's the difference between
luck and Good Luck?"

Max meditated before answering.

"When your family received the inheritance, you
were lucky. But that kind of luck does not depend on
us; that's why it doesn't last long. You just had a bit
of luck, and that's why you don't have much now.
Luck, plain luck, does not depend on you. Good

Luck depends only on you. True luck is the latter. The first, plain luck, simply doesn't exist."

Jim could not believe what he was hearing.

"Are you telling me you don't believe in luck?"

"Well, if you prefer, we can agree that it does exist, but it is unlikely to happen to us—and when it does, it doesn't last. Did you know that almost 90 percent of people who've won the lottery have gone broke or back to where they were in less than ten years? Good Luck, on the other hand, can happen every time you put your mind to it. That's why it's called Good Luck, because it is the Good one, the real one."

"Why is it the real one? What's the difference?" asked Jim.

"Do you want to hear the story?" said Max.

Jim hesitated. Even if he couldn't go back in time, he had nothing to lose by listening. He also found it amusing that his childhood friend would want to tell him a story at age sixty-four. It had been a very long time since anybody had talked to him as if he were a young boy.

"All right, tell me the story," Jim agreed.

First Rule of Good Luck

Luck doesn't last long,
because it does not depend on you.
Good Luck is created by each of us:
that's why it lasts forever.

Part Two

The Legend of the Magic Clover

Merlin's Challenge

A long time ago, in a very distant kingdom, Merlin the wizard gathered all the knights in the area. He took them to the castle's gardens and told them:

"For a long time, many of you have asked me for a challenge. Some of you have suggested I organize a tournament among all the knights in the kingdom. Others have asked that I hold a contest to prove your ability with the spear and sword. However, I am going to propose a different challenge."

Expectations were very high. Merlin continued:

"I have heard that in our kingdom, seven days from today, a *Magic Clover* will grow."

The knights whispered to one another. They felt restless. Some knew what he was talking about. Others didn't. Merlin shushed them all.

"Be calm! Be calm! Let me explain what the *Magic Clover* is. It is the only four-leaf clover that gives its owner a unique power: *unlimited luck*. No limits in time or space. It brings luck in combat, in business, in love, in riches . . . luck with no limits!"

The knights talked among themselves once again with great excitement. They all wanted to find the *four-leaf Magic Clover*. Some even stood up, crying out shouts of victory.

Again, Merlin managed to calm them down and continued:

"Be calm! Be calm! I haven't told you everything yet. The *four-leaf Clover* will grow in the Enchanted

22

Forest, beyond the twelve hills, behind the Valley
of Oblivion. I have no idea about the exact
place, but somewhere in the Forest, the *Clover*
will appear."

All the excitement the knights had shown at the
beginning vanished. First there was silence, then
sighs of discouragement were heard. The Enchanted
Forest was as big as all the inhabited area of the
kingdom. It comprised thousands and thousands of
acres of thick forest. How could a tiny four-leaf
clover be found in such a vast area? Finding a needle
in a barn would have been a thousand times easier!
At least the latter would have been a reasonable
challenge.

Facing such an impossible challenge, most of the
knights started to leave the royal castle, groaning
and looking with disapproval at Merlin as they filed
past him.

"Let me know when you have a reasonable
challenge," said one.

"Had I known, I wouldn't have bothered to come," said someone else.

"What a challenge! Why didn't you send us to a desert to find a blue grain of sand? That would have been easier," said another knight ironically.

One after another, all the knights left the garden and returned to their horses. At last only two knights were left.

"Well?" asked Merlin. "You are not leaving?"

One of the two knights, whose name was Nott and who wore a black cape, said:

"I know it will be difficult. The Enchanted Forest is huge. But I know someone who can help me. I think I can find that clover. I will look for the *four-leaf Magic Clover*. The clover will be mine."

The other knight, whose name was Sid and who wore a white cape, remained in silence, until Merlin looked at him, trying to find out what he was thinking. Then he said:

"If you say that the *four-leaf Magic Clover,* the clover of unlimited luck, will be found in the forest, I believe it shall be that way. I trust you. That's why I shall go to the forest."

So being, both knights headed toward the Enchanted Forest, Nott riding his black horse and Sid riding his white horse.

Second Rule of Good Luck

Many are those
who want Good Luck,
but few are those
willing to pursue it.

The Gnome,
Prince of the Earth

Traveling through the kingdom to reach the Enchanted Forest was treacherous and draining, and it took both knights two days to reach the place. That left only five days to find the *Magic Clover*. They had no time to waste. However, both knights decided to rest and begin their search the next morning.

The knights had traveled separately and did not meet in any of the stops they made to rest or to let their horses drink. Neither of them knew where the other was in the forest.

The forest was very dark. It was dark even during the day because the thick and huge tree canopy blocked the sun. The night was cold and silent. The inhabitants of the Enchanted Forest were aware of the presence of the two newcomers.

The next day, very early in the morning, Nott was already looking for the clover in the forest. And this was his first thought:

"The *Magic Clover* will grow from the soil. And who is it that best knows each and every palm of ground in the Enchanted Forest? That's easy: The Prince of the Earth. In other words, the Gnome. The Gnome lives underground and has built tunnels and corridors throughout the Enchanted Forest. He will tell me where the *four-leaf Magic Clover* will grow."

So Nott, the knight with the black cape and black horse, asked all the strange creatures he met on his way where the Gnome was to be found, until, finally, he met him.

"What is it that you want?" asked the Gnome. "People have been telling me you've been looking for me all day long."

"That's right," answered Nott as he got off his horse. "I have been told that five days from today, a *four-leaf Magic Clover* will grow in the forest. And clover can only grow from the soil, so you, Prince of the Earth, must know where it will grow. You are the only one who knows each millimeter of soil under this immense forest. You know better than anyone the roots of all the plants, bushes, and trees that grow in this forest. If the *four-leaf Magic Clover* is going to grow five days from today, you must have seen its roots already. Tell me where it is."

"Hmmm," meditated the Gnome.

"You know as well as I," continued Nott, "that the *Magic Clover* brings unlimited luck only to knights, so it is of no value to you, since you are a gnome, or to any of the inhabitants of the Enchanted Forest. Tell me where it will grow. I know you know."

"I know the power of the *four-leaf Magic Clover*. And I have all the luck I need as Prince of the Earth; you'd be welcome to the clover if you could find it. But I have not seen its roots anywhere in the forest. In fact, clover has never grown in the Enchanted Forest. It is *impossible* that this clover will grow here. Whoever told you so has probably lied to you."

"Are you sure you're not the liar? I hope you have not told Sid, the knight with the white cape and white horse, where the clover will grow!" exclaimed Nott angrily.

"I don't know what you're talking about! I don't know who Sid is, and I have no idea who has told you this nonsense. Not a single clover plant has ever grown in this forest, not even clover with three leaves. Quite simply, clover doesn't grow in this forest because it can't. So leave me alone. I have lived in this forest for over a hundred and fifty years and no one ever asked me such a stupid question. And now, good-bye to you!"

Nott, the knight with the black cape, realized it would be useless to insist. So he mounted his horse, turned around, and decided to wait until the next day. After all, Gnome could be right and Merlin might have been wrong in the place or the timing.

At that moment, Nott felt how people feel when they are told that luck is not on their side: He felt some fear. But the easiest thing to do is to substitute skepticism: to tell yourself, "That simply can't be." That's the reply that makes the fear of having no luck recede. And that's exactly what Nott thought. That's why he decided not to listen to the Gnome. Nott would spend some time refusing to believe what the Gnome had told him. He would do just that during the next day.

Meanwhile, on the morning of the third day, Sid, the knight in the white cape, had the same exact idea that Nott had had. He also knew that the Gnome was the one to ask where the *Magic Clover* would grow. All day long he tried to find him. He asked many strange creatures and finally found the Gnome just a few minutes after Nott had left him grumbling at one of the entrances of his cavern, with its infinite corridors.

"Are you the Gnome of the Enchanted Forest, the one they call Prince of the Earth?" Sid asked, as he got off his horse.

"Yes, that's me. Oh boy, another enlightened mind! And what is it that you want?"

"Well, you see, I have been told that five days from today, a *four-leaf Magic Clover* will grow in the forest and—" Sid could not finish his sentence. The Gnome turned as red as a tomato and breathed in air, making his chest and face look like they were going to blow up.

"What on Earth is the deal with this *Magic Clover?* I already told the other knight: There-have-never-been-magic-clovers-in-this-forest: Clover cannot grow in this forest, it's that simple. Whoever told you it can is wrong. Or he is tricking you, or maybe he had too much to drink. You are better off returning to your castle or rescuing some lady who might be in danger. You are wasting your time here."

Sid figured out that something was going on: according to Merlin, the *Magic Clover* would grow in the forest, and according to the Gnome, it was impossible that under the given conditions any clover could ever grow in the Enchanted Forest. Both were probably telling the truth. So to keep on looking for the *Magic Clover* was a waste of time. If under the given conditions no clover could grow there, the thing to do was to find out what was needed for

clover to grow. And so Sid asked the Gnome as he
tried to appease him:

"Hold on, hold on. Are you saying that clover has
never grown . . . anywhere in the Enchanted
Forest?"

"Never! Never indeed!" insisted the Gnome,
grumbling as he walked toward his home.

"Don't leave, don't leave just yet, please. Tell me
why. I want to know why clover has never grown in
the forest."

The Gnome turned around and answered:

"It is the soil. Obviously, the reason is the soil. No
one has ever changed this soil. Nobody has ever
bothered to work this soil, to improve it. Clover
needs new soil to grow and the soil in this forest has
never been renewed. It has always been the same.
How do you expect clover to grow here?"

"Therefore, Gnome, Prince of the Earth, if I wanted to have a chance, just one chance to see a clover plant grow in the forest . . . should I *renew* the soil, should I *change* it?"

"Of course. Don't you know that you achieve new things only when you do new things? If the soil doesn't change, things will remain the same: no clover will grow."

"And do you know where I could find some new soil?"

The Gnome had almost entirely disappeared into his den and his hand was about to close the wooden door that communicated with the world above. But he answered Sid:

"There's some new soil close to the land of the Cowls, just a few miles from here. It is virgin soil that has never been used. The Cowls, the dwarf cows with twelve legs, use that soil as a privy, so it is full of manure. That really is good fresh soil."

The knight thanked the Gnome effusively. He
mounted his white horse with enthusiasm and
quickly rode to the land of the Cowls. He knew his
chances were slim but at least it was a *step forward*.

He reached the land of the Cowls at sunset. Finding
the soil that the Gnome described was easy. It really
was fresh soil, clean and pure, and one could tell it
was rich in nutrients. He was only able to fill two
bags, the two attached to his saddle. But that was
enough to cover a small plot of land.

Soon after that, Sid headed toward a quiet place in
the forest far from any village with his two bags of
new soil. The chosen place seemed right. He tore
out all the weeds. Then he dug the old soil, the soil
that had never been *changed*, the original soil,
and removed it. And finally, he applied the fresh,
new soil.

When he finished, he went to sleep. He had only
brought enough soil to cover a few feet. Would that
be the chosen place, the place where the *Magic*

Clover would grow? Being realistic, he thought it seemed *impossible* to be so lucky. Just a few feet out of millions of acres was like having one chance in a hundred billion. Nevertheless, he had done something important: *he had done something different,* something never done in the forest before. If there had never been clover, if nobody had ever found it, it was because all those who had tried had done the same exact things, the things that everyone had done before. Being a true knight, he knew that *doing things differently* was the first step toward success.

Still, he knew that the odds were bad: would the place he had chosen to put the fresh soil he brought be the spot where the *four-leaf Magic Clover* would grow? But at least he had learned one reason that explained the absence of clover. And he would learn still more the next day. He was sure of that.

Lying down, resting his head on the ground, Sid looked at the soil he had just applied. He thought that the Gnome was telling *his* truth. He also thought that Merlin told *his* truth. Those were two truths that apparently contradicted each other, but, after acting as he had, applying new soil to the original soil, the contradiction disappeared. "Just because there has been no clover in the past, doesn't necessarily mean that there can't be any in the future, now that the soil conditions are different," he thought.

He fell asleep imagining clover germinating from the new soil he had applied. Dreaming about this helped him forget how unlikely it was that those few feet of soil were the ones chosen by destiny to welcome the *Magic Clover.*

Night came. Only four days were left.

Third Rule of Good Luck

If you have no Good Luck now,
it might be because you're
under the usual conditions.
To have Good Luck,
you must create
new conditions.

The Lady of the Lake

The fourth morning was colder than usual. The singing of the goldfinches, robins, blackbirds, mockingbirds, and swallows finally muted the sound of the crickets.

Nott mounted his horse after eating some wild strawberries. He was not optimistic. The information that the Gnome had given him truly made him

worry. Literally: *"Clover cannot grow in the forest."*
Not only that, he had also said that not a single clover
plant had ever grown in the entire Enchanted Forest.
And the Gnome knew what he was talking about.

Still, Nott thought that maybe the Gnome was lying.
He told himself he had not been told the truth. Even
if thinking that way led him nowhere, at least it
calmed him down. He decided to spend the day
looking for someone who would disagree with the
information that the Gnome had given him. That
would bring him luck once more.

After riding his horse for more than five hours, Nott
the knight heard the sound of a stream nearby. Since
he was feeling thirsty and imagined his horse was
thirsty too, he followed the sound of the water until
he reached a great lake.

The lake was very beautiful. It was full of water lilies
with red and white flowers. He drank a bit and sat by
the lake, while his horse drank eagerly. Suddenly, a
voice behind him got him on his feet.

"Who are you?" It was a feminine voice, sweet but deep, fragile but firm, seductive but defiant. He turned and saw the Lady of the Lake.

The Lady of the Lake was amazing. She was a woman of a beauty and perfection never seen before, her body shaped by water rising from the lake and still part of it.

Nott had heard about her. He quickly realized that he could get some information from her about his impossible mission.

"I am Nott, the knight of the black cape."

"What are you and your black horse doing next to my lake? You already drank. Now what do you want? You are waking up my water lilies. And this is their nap time. My water lilies sleep during the day and sing at night. If you wake them up, they won't sing tonight. Their singing absorbs the water in the lake during the night. If the water lilies don't sing, the water in the lake doesn't evaporate, and if the water doesn't evaporate, the lake will overflow, and if the lake causes a flood, many flowers, plants, and trees will drown and die. So hush up, keep quiet, and go away! Don't you wake up my water lilies!"

"Hold it, hold it," interrupted the knight. "I'm not interested in your problems. I will leave soon. I just want to ask you something. You, Lady of the Lake, you who distribute the water through all the Enchanted Forest, you, who water all the corners of this forest, tell me: where does clover grow in this forest?"

The Lady started to laugh. She laughed mockingly but also with joy. It was a loud and yet discreet laughter. High-pitched but also deep. When she finished laughing, she put on a serious face and said:

"No clover can grow in this forest. Can't you see that the water I distribute reaches all the forest through filtration? My water doesn't follow any rivers or streams, it is filtered through the walls of

44

the lake to every corner of the Enchanted Forest. Have you seen puddles anywhere in the forest? Clover needs lots of water. It needs a stream that will continuously supply water. You will never find clover in this forest."

The Lady of the Lake disappeared in the water. Amazing. The water vapor that gave her human form lost its shape and simply fell to the surface of the lake in the form of thousands of water drops.

Nott hardly paid attention to the marvelous appearance he had just witnessed. He was tired of hearing the same story. He remained very serious and thoughtful. What was going on? He started to realize that surely *he was not going to have any luck*. This caused him great fear, greater than the fear he had felt after talking to the Gnome.

"I must find someone to tell me otherwise. I must find someone to tell me that luck, the *Magic Clover*, can grow in the Enchanted Forest," he repeated to himself.

He started to hate luck. It was abominable. It was the most desirable thing yet the most inaccessible thing in this world. And he could not stand feeling this way. Waiting for luck brought him great dismay, but that was the only thing he could do. What else could he do?

So Nott mounted his horse and rode with no set route for the rest of the day all over the Enchanted Forest, hoping to be lucky enough to find the *four-leaf Magic Clover.*

That day, Sid the knight had woken up a bit later than the day before. He had stayed up late the night preparing the fresh, new soil, so he had decided to sleep just one more hour.

He thought of things to do that day, as he shared an apple with his white horse.

"I already have the soil," he said to himself. "Now I need to know how much water it needs. The chances I chose the correct spot are very low. I know that. But if I have been *lucky,* and this is the *right* spot . . . then I must make sure that the soil gets the right amount of water."

He didn't think twice. Any knight knew that the best water in the Enchanted Forest, without a doubt, belonged to the Lady of the Lake.

It took him quite some time to find the lake. He had to ask the most unfriendly, the meanest animals he had met so far in the forest.

He reached the lake just a few minutes after Nott had left. He approached the lake very, very slowly. He walked without making any noise, but then, by accident, stepped on a red and yellow snail that made a crushing sound. Instantly, the Lady of the Lake emerged stunningly from the lake. She complained once more:

"What are you and your white horse doing next to my lake? What is it that you want? You are waking up my water lilies. And this is their nap time. My water lilies sleep during the day and sing at night. If you wake them up they won't sing tonight. Their singing absorbs the water in the lake during the night. If the water lilies don't sing, the water doesn't evaporate, and if the water doesn't evaporate, the lake will overflow, and if the lake floods, many flowers, plants, and trees will drown and die. So hush up, keep quiet, and go away! Don't you wake up my water lilies!"

Sid was overwhelmed. Not only by the awesome appearance he had just witnessed but also by the problem that the Lady of the Lake presented him. Sid needed to collect water for the spot he had chosen, but he would wake the water lilies if he spent all day getting water from the lake.

Things were getting complicated. There wasn't any more water anywhere else in the Enchanted Forest. Oh well, what could he do? In any case, *he had tried his best*. Since he didn't know what to do for the rest of the day, he took interest in the Lady of the Lake's problem. Maybe he could be of some help.

"Why is there no water coming out of the lake? All lakes let water out."

"Because I . . . , because I . . . ," for the first time, the Lady of the Lake's voice expressed no contrasts, it was a sad voice. It was a painful voice. "Because in my lake," she said, "there is no continuity. There are no rivers that originate from me. On me, water only falls down or flows in. I only receive water, but no streams originate within me. That's why I always have to make sure that the water lilies sleep so they can sing at night. I don't sleep during the day to make sure the water lilies can sleep and during the night, their singing keeps me awake. I am a slave to my water. Please, go away and do not wake up my water lilies."

Sid realized that what the lake was missing was precisely what he needed: a stream.

"I can help you," Sid told her. "But tell me something: Do you know how much water clover needs?" The Lady of the Lake answered:

"It needs plenty of water. It needs a direct source of water, water from a stream. The soil where clover grows needs to be flooded."

"In that case, yes, in that case, I can help you and you can help me!"

"Shushhh! Don't yell so much, you already woke up a water lily. Tell me how."

"If you let me dig a furrow originating from the lake, creating a stream, no more water will accumulate within you. I will make no noise. I will just dig a furrow on the ground and water will flow from the lake. That way, you won't have to worry about your water lilies anymore. You will be able to sleep whenever you want."

The Lady of the Lake seemed to be thinking. Finally, she agreed.

"All right. But don't make any noise." Instantly, the Lady of the Lake disappeared, to Sid's astonishment.

Wasting no time, he used his sword as a hoe, attaching it to the back of his horse. He rode back toward the chosen spot. As he rode, the sword made a deep ditch and water followed it, relieving the lake of its heavy load. Water reached the fresh, new soil. Sid had been successful: he had been able to flood his little plot of land by creating a direct stream that had never existed before.

He went to sleep by the new space he had created. He thought about what had just happened and remembered what his mentor had always told him:

Life gives you back what you give others. Other people's problems are often part of your solution. If you share, you always get more. And that was exactly what had happened: he was willing to forget about the water so as not to wake the water lilies, and it was precisely when he tried to understand the Lady of the Lake's problem that he realized that they both needed the same thing.

Curiously, Sid felt less worried about whether or not the spot he had chosen would be the place where the *Magic Clover* would grow. He might have felt a bit stupid exerting so much effort and caring for the needs of a clover plant, in a place where it *probably* wouldn't grow. But this was not the case. The assurance of knowing that he was doing what he should, made the idea of whether or not he had been *lucky* in choosing the right spot less important. Why? He didn't know. Probably, watering was the right thing to do after applying *new* soil. He was doing what he had to do. And that made him feel better, more so than knowing whether he had chosen the right spot or not.

Indeed, he was aware of the low probability that the place he had chosen to add the new soil and apply plenty of water would be the growing spot of the *four-leaf Magic Clover*. But he already knew two reasons why clover had never grown in the forest. And he would know more the next day. He was sure of that.

Resting his head on the ground, trying to fall asleep, Sid looked at his new soil being watered by the stream. One more night, he visualized the *Magic Clover* germinating and growing upward. That made him happy.

Night came. Only three days were left.

Fourth Rule of Good Luck

Finding new conditions for Good Luck
does not mean looking
for our own benefit only.
Creating conditions,
helping others,
makes Good Luck more likely to appear.

The Sequoia, Queen of the Trees

The next morning, Nott, the knight of the black cape, woke up quite discouraged. According to the information provided by the Gnome and the Lady of the Lake, he was, simply put, wasting his time. Was it worth continuing? Nott the knight was thinking about quitting. However, the journey to reach the Enchanted Forest had been long, and since he was there, he decided to stay until the end.

Nott didn't know what to do. Who could he talk to now? He wandered the forest riding his horse, not knowing where to go. He met all kinds of strange creatures, even those that were supposed to be one of a kind, unique in the Enchanted Forest. But he found no clover.

As he rode, he never took his eyes off the ground, looking for any sign that might show him where the *four-leaf Magic Clover* could grow. Suddenly, he realized that he hadn't talked to Sequoia, the first inhabitant of the Enchanted Forest. She would know something.

He rode to the exact center of the forest. Sequoia was the first tree born in the Enchanted Forest, that's why she was right in the center. Nott got off his horse and walked toward her. He knew that in the Enchanted Forest, all living creatures, and even many of the inert objects, could talk. So he addressed the Sequoia, saying:

"Sequoia, Queen of the Trees, can you talk?"

There was no response. Nott the knight tried once more.

"Sequoia, Queen of the Trees, I'm talking to you. Please answer me. Don't you know who I am? I am Nott, the knight."

Sequoia started to move her trunk and answered the knight:

"I already know who you are. Don't you know I know all the trees in this forest? Don't you know that through our leaves, all, and I mean absolutely all the trees in this forest are physically in contact with each other? Information travels fast through our branches. Ask me something if you wish, but then leave. I am tired. I'm over two thousand years old. Talking makes me tired."

"I'll be brief," answered Nott. "I have been told that three days from today, the *four-leaf Magic Clover* of unlimited luck will grow in the Enchanted Forest. But both the Gnome and the Lady of the Lake have told me that clover has never grown in the Enchanted Forest. You have lived in the forest since its creation. You know everything that goes on here because you have talked and still talk to all the trees in the forest. My question is very simple: Is it true that clover has never grown in this forest?"

Sequoia took her time. She went through her memories, two thousand years back, going through each year of her life that was stored in each of the two thousand rings that made up the inside of her wide trunk. This took time. Minutes went by and Nott the knight grew impatient:

"Come on, answer me. I'm in a hurry," he complained.

"I'm thinking. I'm trying to remember. You are impatient, like most humans. You should be like the trees, full of patience."

About five more minutes went by. Nott the knight, losing his patience, turned around, believing that

Sequoia was refusing to answer. But she started to talk, just when Nott was about to mount his horse again. Like a librarian who had reviewed two thousand files of the books in her library, looking for a specific book, Sequoia answered once she had finished her search:

"It is true. Clover has never grown in the Enchanted Forest. And especially a *four-leaf Magic Clover*. Never in these two thousand years. Never."

Nott felt desolate. Merlin had probably got the wrong information. Or even worse . . . the idea that Merlin had tricked him started to seep into his every bone.

Nott felt really depressed. That was the third inhabitant to tell him there would be no luck for him. He was so obsessed with that reality, that he couldn't see beyond it. Surely, hearing others say what one already knows leads nowhere except to the confirmation of that evidence. Anyone as obsessed as Nott was with knowing whether or not there are any clover plants in the forest cannot think of anything but that. He cannot realize that it is necessary to *do* something about it. So Nott was miserable.

Sid the knight woke up that morning more satisfied than the day before. He thought about everything he had achieved: new soil and plenty of water. If that was the spot where the *Magic Clover* would grow, now he needed to know what degree of sunshine and what degree of shade was required.

Sid was a knight, not a gardening expert, so he needed to talk to a wise person who knew about plants and trees. The knight asked himself who he could ask about this subject. Suddenly it dawned on him:

"Of course! That's it! Sequoia. She is the wisest tree in the forest. She will know how much sunlight clover needs!"

Sid rode his horse to the center of the Enchanted Forest. He got off his horse and approached the tree, just as Nott had done a short time ago.

"Distinguished Sequoia, Queen of the Trees, do you wish to talk?"

Again, there was no response. Sid the knight insisted.

"Respected and venerable Sequoia, Queen of the Trees, if you are not too tired, I would like to ask you something. If you cannot talk now, I will come back at a later time."

In fact, Sequoia had decided not to answer a second arrogant knight who had come to ask her impertinent questions, but she could see that Sid was

not an impatient or arrogant knight, judging by his
kind words and his respectful gesture, kneeling
before her with his head down. As Sid got ready to
leave, Sequoia addressed him:

"Indeed, I am tired. But tell me, what is your
question?"

"Thank you for answering me, Queen of the Trees.
My question is very simple: how much sunlight does
a clover plant need to grow, if there's good fresh soil
and the right amount of water?"

"Hmmm," Sequoia meditated. But this time she
took little time to answer since she knew the answer
perfectly. "It needs sunlight as well as shade. But you
won't find such a place in this forest. This forest is
shade everywhere you go, as you have observed
yourself. That's why no clover has ever grown here.
That's the answer to your question. Take care now
and farewell."

But Sid the knight could not be easily discouraged.

"Hold on, hold on. Just one more question, I beg you. Queen of the Trees, would you allow me to prune some branches off some of your subjects? Do I have your consent?"

Sequoia replied:

"You don't need my consent. You just need to remove the dead branches and the dry leaves. No one has ever bothered to keep the trees in this forest clean and healthy. No one has ever pruned our branches. That's why there's no light in the forest. The inhabitants of this forest are very lazy. They just loaf around and leave everything 'for tomorrow.' If you work just a bit, you'll be able to get the same amount of light and shade under any tree. You just need to get rid of the dead leaves and branches. You don't need my permission. Any tree will be delighted if you do that for him."

"Thank you. Many thanks," said Sid. He got up and, walking backward respectfully, mounted his horse again.

The knight of the white horse rode swiftly until he reached the place where he had applied new soil and had made the water available. It was getting late. What if he cleared the branches off the trees the next day? In fact, nothing else had to be done: he had the soil, water, and right amount of light.

He could rest now and devote the last day to pruning the trees. But Sid remembered Sequoia's words. People were always leaving things for tomorrow. And he also remembered some advice that had always worked for him: "Act now and don't postpone things." It was true that there seemed to be nothing left to do and that he could spend his last day pruning. But if he did it at once, he would have an extra day and having an extra day could prove useful. So he took advantage of the hours of daylight left to prune the branches and leaves.

Faithful to his principles, he decided to *act* and not *postpone* the things that had to be done.

He climbed each of the tree tops in the chosen area. He couldn't be sure where the rays of sun would enter, and not wanting to take any risks, he cleared more than twelve of the giant trees, one by one.

The trees were many feet tall and he had to climb them each with the little rope he had with him. He had to get rid of the dead branches and leaves with his sword, since he didn't have the right tools. He worked all through the night, giving himself to this task as if the only thing that mattered in that moment was to prune these trees. The results were excellent.

He was really happy. Curiously enough, he no longer thought about whether or not the place he had chosen to add new soil, to flood with water, and to clear of branches would be the growing place of the *four-leaf Magic Clover.* He now knew all the requirements of clover and had provided them. How would he spend his next day? Maybe there was something else that was indispensable. He had worked all night long just in case.

One more time, Sid visualized his *Magic Clover*. This time he imagined it well rooted in the humid soil of the small space that he had created. He imagined its four leaves, shaped like little hearts, open to receive the rays of sun that penetrated through the branches of the gigantic trees that surrounded it.

He couldn't explain why but the more he knew about the conditions needed for a *Magic Clover* to grow, the less he worried about whether or not his place would be the one where the *Clover* would grow.

Only two days were left.

Fifth Rule of Good Luck

If you postpone
the creation of new conditions,
Good Luck never arrives.
Creating new conditions
is sometimes hard work, but . . .
do it today!

Ston, the Mother of All Rocks

On the sixth day, Nott wandered with sadness through the Enchanted Forest. Surely, he didn't think he would find any clover, but he didn't want to go back to the palace alone. If he was going to make a fool of himself, he would rather share that experience with Sid.

The sixth day was the most boring Nott spent in the forest. He hunted quite a few strange creatures and came across some unique plants he had never seen before, but other than that, nothing worth telling took place.

The worst thing was how he felt about something he had learned, something that brought him great sadness: he was sure he would have no luck in life. Otherwise, he would have found the *Magic Clover* by now. Unless, of course, Merlin had tricked him.

But if Merlin had tricked him, why not return to the castle? Why did he keep waiting?

To wait was to trust Merlin, hoping to have luck, but, at this point, it only proved that luck was not on its way. What was he doing wrong? Why did he feel so miserable? "I deserve luck. Why doesn't it come?" Nott asked himself.

This is how the knight of the black horse and black cape spent the rest of the day. Since he had nothing else to do, he decided to talk to Ston, the Mother of

All Rocks. He wanted to confirm with one more person what he already knew: that no clover would grow in the Enchanted Forest; that he was a man with no luck.

It is no wonder that Nott would do that, since that's one of the characteristics of people who think that they have no luck. They look for other people who will confirm their way of thinking. Feeling like a victim is not a pleasant feeling, but it does free you from the responsibility of misfortune.

Ston stood on top of the Boulder of Boulders, an inhospitable mountain made only of rock. Climbing it was a tough job. From its top he could see most of the Enchanted Forest. Maybe he'd spot Sid and be able to talk to him, and find out if he wanted to go back home.

When he reached the top, he met Ston, the Mother of All Rocks, who was talking to a twelve-winged bird. As soon as Nott was visible, the bird flew away and Ston said to him:

"Look at that! Here comes one of these knights who roams around looking for clover. For the past four days, you have been the main topic in the forest. Have you found the *Magic Clover?*" She smiled mockingly at him.

"You know I haven't," answered Nott, visibly angry. "Tell me, Ston, isn't it true that there isn't and has never been a *four-leaf Magic Clover* in this forest? Or is there one around here, among these stones? I doubt it, right?"

The Mother of All Rocks couldn't stop laughing.

"Of course not! How do you expect clover to grow on stones? I can tell that you are starting to lose your mind after so many days wandering in the Enchanted Forest. You should be careful . . . if you spend too much time here, you will go crazy, like most humans who have wandered round this forest with no set goal. No, there are no clover plants here. *Four-leaf Magic Clovers* cannot grow where there are stones."

Nott descended the Boulder of all Boulders slowly, as he heard Ston roar with laughter.

There was nothing he could do about it. His fear had finally been confirmed. "I will have no luck," he thought. Then, he remembered Sid, and cheered up as he thought: "That lunatic won't find the *Magic Clover* either, no matter how much he clomps around this forest." Thinking about Sid's failure calmed him down, comforted him, even made him feel good. "If there's no *Magic Clover* for me, there won't be any for him, either," he said with confidence, loud and clear.

He then mounted his horse and left in search of a place to sleep.

Sid, on the other hand, upon waking up, noticed that the work he had done the night before had been worth it: he saw how the rays of sun lit up the fresh soil he had applied the first day, and was able to verify, much to his satisfaction, that both sunlight and shade equally covered each palm of soil that he had prepared. He felt proud of himself. He was happy. He had applied new soil, he had cleared the tree tops to let the rays of sun reach the ground, he had flooded the area with water. Now it was just a matter of having chosen the right spot, but he no longer worried about this.

This was the last day, so it was important to decide how to spend it. Since he had done everything that he considered *necessary*, the smart thing to do was to find out if anything else had been left undone. As he often said, the glass was half full. Now it would have to be filled completely, just in case he had chosen the right spot where the *Magic Clover* would grow, as Merlin had predicted. He had thought about it the night before: he needed to figure out if there was anything indispensable.

Soil, water, sunshine . . . but, what else could be needed?

So he spent his sixth day asking all the creatures he met in the forest if there was anything required for a *four-leaf Clover* to grow, besides soil, water, shade, and sunshine. But nobody was able to tell him if anything else was needed.

It was already noon, and he could not think of anyone else to ask. He needed inspiration, so he decided to visit the highest point in the forest, to see if from there, he could find anything else that might be needed.

All knights knew that the highest point in the forest was the Boulder of Boulders, but as he reached the mountain, he noticed its great elevation. There was only half a day until Merlin's deadline. Was it worth climbing the mountain? Even if he found inspiration there, he wouldn't have much time left to do anything.

Still, he decided to climb. Why? Simply because *he thought of what he had done* and the effort it had entailed. After all he had achieved, it made no sense not to go all the way.

He climbed the mountain and enjoyed a gentle breeze. When he made it to the top, he sat down and observed, scanning the horizon in search of inspiration. But nothing happened.

Suddenly, a voice startled him. It came from. . . under his rear end! It was Ston, the Mother of All Rocks.

"You are squashing me!"

Sid jumped so fast that he almost fell down the slope of the rocks.

"A stone that talks? That's unbelievable!"

"I'm not a talking stone: I am Ston, the Mother of All Rocks," she corrected him, noticeably annoyed. "I presume you are the other knight who is searching for the . . . ha, ha, ha! . . . *Magic Clover.*"

"Are you really the Mother of All Rocks? In that case . . . you probably don't know much about clover, right?"

"Of course I don't know much about clover, but some things I do know," she answered. "I already told the other knight wearing black: no *four-leaf Clover* can grow wherever there are stones."

"You said *four-leaf Clover?*" asked Sid.

"Yes, *four-leaf Clover.*"

"What about clover with three leaves?" he asked.

"Yes, three-leaved clover can grow on a soil that has stones. But *four-leaf Clover* grows weaker on a stony soil and this is why it requires a soil completely free of stones so it won't prevent the plants from growing."

This appreciation—comparing the needs of clover with three leaves and clover with four leaves—would have appeared to be of very little importance to most people, but not to Sid. He knew that what really matters is to know things that other people don't. He knew that often, the key elements can only be found in the small details. One can never find the answer to the "apparently unnecessary, but indispensable" in the obvious.

"Of course! How could I not have realized before? Thanks a lot! I must leave, time is running out."

Sid descended the Boulder of Boulders as fast as he could. He had to race to the chosen spot: He had not removed the stones.

When he got there, he still had two more hours of sunlight. Sid got rid of all the stones one by one. In fact, the area he had chosen was full of stones. If, by any chance, he had chosen the right spot, the *Magic Clover* would not have grown there because of the stones.

Sid realized the importance of thinking of the glass as being almost full, in order to help him concentrate on filling it. This had always helped him to look ahead. Sid also realized that there is vital information in small details. Even when things seem to be all done, if one has the right attitude, willing to know if there's anything else that can be done, one can always find a hint that will let him know. In fact, that's exactly what had happened. Fortunately he had not delayed the pruning of the branches. If he had postponed that, he would have never known that the stones had to be removed.

One more night, he went to sleep next to the space he had created. And one more night, he imagined the beautiful *Magic Clover* in all its splendor, in the middle of the soil that he had created, lit by the sun, watered, and free of stones. That night, he also imagined taking it in his hands. He felt its smooth texture gently brushing his skin, saw its intense green color as its beautiful leaves unfolded. He even breathed the soothing smell of chlorophyll that the *Magic Clover* gave off. It was all so real that for the first time he felt certain that that would be the place where the *Clover* would grow. He could picture it, he could feel it with extraordinary detail. This made him feel very good.

In any case, he would find out the next day. He was sure of that too.

Night came. Only one more day was left. The day in which the *four-leaf Magic Clover,* the clover of unlimited luck, would be born in the Enchanted Forest.

Sixth Rule of Good Luck

Sometimes, even under the seemingly
right conditions,
Good Luck doesn't arrive.
Look for the
seemingly unnecessary but indispensable
conditions in the small details.

Nott Finds
Sid's Secret Place

The last night should have been calm, but that was not the case for either of the two knights. While Nott looked for a place to sleep, he felt his horse stepping on fresh soil, just watered, free of overhead branches and with no stones. A bit further he saw Sid resting, his horse standing with a rope around a tree.

"Sid!"

Sid got up. He still hadn't fallen asleep.

"Nott! How are things going? Have you found the clover?" asked Sid.

"No. Well, in fact, I haven't even been looking for it these last three days. The very first day, the Gnome told me that there was no clover in the entire forest, so I decided to quit looking."

"In that case," Sid asked, "what the devil are you doing here? Why don't you return to your castle?"

Before he could answer, Nott noticed that Sid's clothing was smeared with the moss that grew on the trunks and his boots were all stained from his last three days of intense work in the Enchanted Forrest. "What happened to you?"

"Since the day the Gnome told me that no clover could grow in the Enchanted Forest, I have spent

time creating this space. Look at it! It has new, fresh soil, and look how rich it is. Follow me! I'll show you the stream that I have dug all the way from the lake where the Lady lives . . . and look, look!" continued Sid, very excited to show someone what he had created, "these are all the stones and branches that I have taken away in just two days, because I don't know if you're aware but, where—"

Nott interrupted him.

"Have you lost your mind? Why on earth have you been working like a beast to make this garden of, of . . . just a few feet, if you don't have the slightest idea where the *Magic Clover* will grow? Don't you realize this forest is millions of times the size of this small plot of land? Are you stupid or what's your problem? Don't you understand there's no point in doing all you've done unless someone tells you where on earth it should be done? You have lost your mind! I'll see you back in town. I'm going to find a quiet place to spend the night."

Nott disappeared into the forest. Sid followed him with his eyes. He was shocked to hear Nott's words. And he thought to himself: "Merlin said that we might find the *Magic Clover,* but he did *not* say that *nothing* had to be done to find it."

Seventh Rule of Good Luck

To those who
only believe in chance,
creating conditions seems absurd.
Those who create conditions
are not worried about
chance.

The Witch and the Owl Visit Nott

The last night should have been placid . . . but that was not the case for either of the two knights . . . once again.

While Nott was sleeping, waiting for the morning light to return to his castle, a noise woke him up so violently that he got on his feet and in just one second drew his sword.

"Whoo, whoooo," the noise came from Morgana's owl. The witch was standing next to him, partially illuminated by the fire that the knight had lit and that was now dying out.

"Who are you? What do you want? Beware, my sword is sharp!"

"Put your sword away. I have come here to make a deal with you, Nott, knight of the black horse and cape."

"A deal? What kind of deal do you want to make? I don't want any deals with any witches, much less with you; you have a terrible reputation."

"Are you sure? It's about . . . a *four-leaf Clover*," Morgana the witch said softly, as she bared her black teeth, rubbed together her ancient hands with their long nails, and wrinkled her sharp and aquiline nose, trying to smile kindly. Nott the knight put his sword away, and stepped forward.

"Let's talk. What do you know?"

"I know where the *four-leaf Magic Clover* will grow."

"Go on! Waste no more time. Tell me," demanded Nott impatiently.

"I will tell you if you first promise to carry out your part of the deal."

"And what is my part of the deal?" asked Nott impatiently.

"I want you to kill Merlin with your sword when you find him!"

"What? Why should I kill Merlin?"

"Because he has tricked you. He, like myself, knows where the *Magic Clover* will grow. The deal is simple: I tell you where to find the *Magic Clover* and you kill Merlin. Unlimited luck for you, and an end to my problems with witchcraft for me. With Merlin's death, you will have access to the *Magic Clover* and I will be rid of my main opponent."

Nott felt so tricked and frustrated, and was so eager to hurt Merlin, that he agreed. This was not strange; when someone has lost faith in creating Good Luck, it seems natural to try to buy it from the first person who offers it. In fact, those who expect to find luck always believe they can find it easily and with no effort. And this is what happened to Nott.

"That's a deal! Tell me where the *Magic Clover* will grow."

"Don't forget you have given me your word. The *Magic Clover* will germinate tomorrow in . . . in the gardens of the king's castle. It will never grow in this forest."

"What?" cried out Nott, disbelieving what he'd just heard.

"Of course! Don't you realize? Merlin tried to trick all knights with his strategy: by proposing the challenge of searching for it in the Enchanted Forest, he meant all the knights to come here and waste their time. Only two of you came. Merlin thought that more would come. But in any case, he managed to keep everyone's attention away from the king's gardens. *Nobody* expects to find the *Magic Clover* there. He will be there tomorrow to pull it out. You must hurry. It took you two days to get here but now you only have one night to get back. Get on your saddle and ride all night long, even if your horse drops dead!"

Nott was furious. At last, all the pieces fit together. That explained why each and every one of the inhabitants of the Enchanted Forest had taken him for a stupid man, spending his time trying to find a *Magic Clover* that would never grow there.

Nott got on his horse and disappeared into the forest at great speed, on his way to the inhabited kingdom, heading to the palace.

Eighth Rule of Good Luck

Nobody can sell Good Luck.
Good Luck cannot be sold.
Do not trust those who sell luck.

The Witch and the Owl Visit Sid

The witch let out a loud and malicious laugh and headed north, where she knew that Sid was spending the night.

Sid was sleeping peacefully—so peacefully that it took the owl three long hoots to wake him up.

"Whoooo, whoooo, whoooo."

"Who's there?" asked Sid as he got on his feet, placing his hand on his sword, ready to draw it.

"Don't be afraid. I am Morgana, the witch."

Sid remained on guard.

"What is it that you want of me?"

The witch was mean. She wanted two things: first, she wanted Nott to kill Merlin, and, second, she wanted to persuade Sid to leave the area, in order to keep the *Magic Clover* in case it grew somewhere in the forest the next day. Morgana made up another lie for Sid.

"The *Magic Clover* will grow tomorrow. But Merlin has lied to you. It is not a clover of unlimited luck . . . it is the clover of misfortune! I myself cast the spell: 'Whoever pulls the clover out, shall die in three days.' But if nobody pulls it out before sunset tomorrow, then Merlin will die that same night. That's why he tricked you and the other knight. To

make sure one of the two of you dies in his place.
Merlin needs the clover to be pulled out tomorrow
before sunset. Return to your castle: Nott has already
returned."

The witch had been very clever: She was leaving Sid,
the knight of the white cape and horse, no options.
If he found the *Magic Clover* the next day, he
wouldn't know what to do. If he pulled it out he
would die. But what if Merlin was right? What if it
was indeed the clover of Good Luck?

The easiest way out was to follow Nott's steps: to
leave the forest without facing the dilemma. He
thought for a few seconds and then told the witch:

"All right. In that case I will set off tonight."

The witch smiled.

"But I will go to see Merlin. I will ask him to pull
the *Magic Clover* out himself. The spell you've told
me about says that whoever pulls it out will die in

three days, but if Merlin does it, he will not die. This way, the spell will be broken, since the person who would die if the clover is not found, and the person who will pull it out and not die are the same person, Merlin. So Merlin will be saved and will give me the *Clover.*"

Sid had outsmarted Morgana the witch, who was no longer smiling. Realizing that Sid had not fallen into her trap, she turned around, her owl resting on her shoulder, got on her broom and left quickly, like a dog with its tail between its legs, grumbling loudly.

Sid thought about what had just happened. He knew that Merlin never tricked anyone. How could Nott have believed such a thing, or anything else that the witch told him? Didn't he know, being a knight, that the truly important thing is not to lose faith in the task at hand?

He had seen so many knights lose hope and quit when Good Luck took its time to make its presence that he had learned the importance of being faithful to what one thought was right.

Before going to sleep, he thought of how important it was not to change one's goal for someone else's goal, in other words, the witch's for his own. Good Luck had always arrived when he had remained faithful to his goal, his task, his mission, and his purpose.

Finally, he remembered what his master had always told him: Do not trust anyone who wants to sell you luck.

Ninth Rule of Good Luck

After creating all the conditions,
be patient, don't quit.
For Good Luck to arrive,
have faith.

The Wind, Lord of Destiny and Luck

The next morning, Sid woke up somewhat restless. He sat close to the spot he had prepared and waited. Hours went by, but nothing happened.

The day took its course, but still nothing happened. Sid said to himself:

"Well, in any case, I have lived with passion these days in the Enchanted Forrest. I have done what I thought was the right and necessary thing. Yes, it was highly unlikely to have chosen the exact spot where the *four-leaf Magic Clover of unlimited luck* would grow."

But all of a sudden, something he couldn't even imagine took place.

The Wind, Lord of Destiny and Luck, he who apparently controls fate, began to stir the leaves of the trees. And soon after that, small seeds that looked like tiny grains of green gold started to fall. They were *four-leaf Clover* seeds, each seed being . . . *a good luck Clover in the making!* It was pouring down . . . not just one *four-leaf Clover* seed but an infinite number of *four-leaf Clover* seeds.

But the truly remarkable thing is that the seeds were falling not only where Sid was standing, but throughout the entire Enchanted Forest, *over absolutely each and every corner* of the forest.

And not just in the Enchanted Forest, but over the entire Kingdom: *four-leaf Clover* seeds fell on the heads of those knights who had not accepted Merlin's challenge. The seeds poured down on all the strange creatures of the forest, on the Gnome, the Sequoia, the Lady of the Lake, old Ston. . . . They fell on Nott and Morgana. *Four-leaf Clover* seeds poured down *everywhere!*

The inhabitants of the Enchanted Forest and the inhabited Kingdom paid no attention to them. They knew that once a year, during that season, this strange green-gold rain, so useless and annoying, poured on them. In fact, each year this event bothered them beyond words, it was such a sticky mess.

Five minutes later, the *four-leaf Clover* seed rain stopped. The tiny green-gold seeds dissolved like snowflakes as they hit the ground. They just died out, like seeds that are sown in the desert.

And the millions of seeds that fell on the Enchanted Forest became sterile as well.

All, except a few hundred seeds that fell on a few
square feet of fresh soil, where there was some
sunshine and some shade, where there was plenty of
water and where it was free of stones.

Those and only those seeds became *four-leaf*
Clovers in a very short time, hundreds of those
Magic Clovers, enough to have luck all year
long . . . until next year's rainfall. In other words,
unlimited luck. Sid remained motionless as he
watched the Good Luck that he had created,
he knelt as a sign of gratitude and tears poured
from his eyes.

When he noticed that the wind was dying down, he
wished to say farewell and offer thanks for bringing
the seeds. So he said:

"Oh Wind, Lord of Destiny and Luck, where are
you? I want to thank you!"

The wind answered:

"You don't need to thank me. Every year, on this same day, I distribute *four-leaf Clover* seeds throughout the Enchanted Forest and over all the corners of the inhabited Kingdom. I am the Lord of Destiny and Luck. Contrary to what many believe, I don't give out luck, I just make sure it is distributed equally. The *Magic Clovers* germinated because you created the right conditions. *Anybody who had done the same would have created Good Luck too.* I just did what I always do. The Good Luck that I carry with me is always there. The problem is that almost everybody thinks that they don't need to do *anything.*"

He continued:

"In fact, the spot you chose made no difference. The important thing was to prepare it the way you did. Luck is the sum of *opportunity* and *preparation*. But the *opportunity* . . . is always there."

And that is what happened indeed.

True enough, *four-leaf Clovers* grew only by Sid's side, because he had been the only one in the entire Kingdom who had created the conditions to keep them from dying.

Contrary to what many people believe, Good Luck is not something that happens to a few who do nothing.

Good Luck is something that can happen to *all* of us, if we *do something*.

And that "something" consists only in creating the conditions as to make sure that those *opportunities*—that exist for all of us—do not die like *four-leaf Clover* seeds falling on sterile ground.

And the wind left, as Sid departed the Enchanted Forest.

Tenth Rule of Good Luck

Creating Good Luck consists in
preparing conditions for opportunity.
But opportunity has
nothing to do with luck or chance:
it is always there.

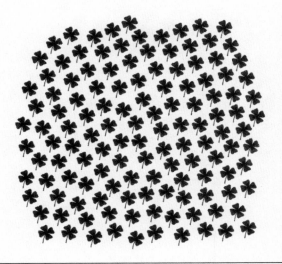

Moral of the Story

Creating Good Luck consists
only in . . .
creating the conditions.

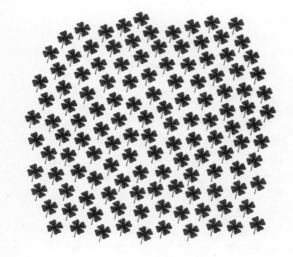

Meeting Merlin Again

Nott rode through the whole seventh night. When he reached the castle, his black horse's flanks were covered with blood, thanks to the blows that his rider had given him with his whip and spurs, in order to get to the royal gardens on time to pull out the *Magic Clover*. When he arrived, the black horse collapsed and died.

Nott stormed through the castle's gate and down
each of its halls, knocking down everything he found
on his way with blows and kicks. He brandished his
sword in one hand, and his face was contorted, his
eyes red-stained with rage.

"Merlin! Merlin! Where are you? Don't you hide,
I will find you."

Nott decided to go where he was sure to
find Merlin: the green and luxuriant garden of
the palace.

When he opened the glass door that led outside,
he saw Merlin standing in the center of the
garden. He stood leaning on his long white cane,
a grave look on his face. But the garden was
no longer a garden: it was a courtyard covered
with tiles. During the last seven days, the builders
of the palace had been busy paving the floor
with tiles.

Nott's sword dropped from his hand.

"Why have you done this? Why have you covered the garden with tiles?" he asked Merlin.

"Because if I hadn't, you would have tried to kill me. You would not have listened to my reasons. It was the only way to make you understand that the witch had lied to you. I, Merlin the Wizard, know everything. I *knew* that the witch would sell you her luck: the luck that seldom follows. And I *knew* that you would come to kill me—and that only after looking for it for many hours would you be sure that the *Magic Clover* was not here. I had to stop you from doing that."

Nott began to comprehend his great mistake. He had wanted everything to be easy. He had always thought that he *deserved* to be lucky. At that precise moment, in the castle's garden, standing next to Merlin, he realized that he was wrong. Merlin continued:

"Now you know: the *Magic Clover* is not here. It germinated in the Enchanted Forest just a few hours ago, just as I promised. There were plenty of *Magic Clovers*, even for you. But you quit: you lost confidence in yourself. Not only that: you always expected others to give you luck."

Nott turned around, and without a horse or sword, returned to his castle where he lived alone for the rest of his days.

The next day, Sid reached the town. The first thing he did was to head to the palace to tell Merlin that he had found the *Magic Clover, the clover of unlimited luck.* He wanted to thank him.

"Merlin! Merlin! Look!" He showed him a handful of *four-leaf Clovers, clovers of Good Luck.* "I came to thank you. I owe this to you."

"Not at all!" replied Merlin. "I didn't do anything. I did absolutely nothing." He continued. "It was *you* who decided to go to the Enchanted Forest, *you* accepted the challenge among hundreds of knights, *you* decided to add fresh, new soil, even after being told that no clover would ever grow in the forest. *You* decided to share your luck with the Lady of the Lake, thus *changing more than one thing*. It was *you* who decided to persevere and not delay the pruning of the branches. *You* were the one who went beyond to find the *seemingly unnecessary* and realized the importance of getting rid of the stones even after everything looked ready. *You* had the necessary *faith* to *believe*. *You* were the one who had confidence in what you had done, even when they tried to sell you luck."

And Merlin added:

"But the most important thing, Sid: *It was you who did not expect to find the Clover just by chance. You created the conditions to make it come your way.*"

He concluded by stating:

"You chose to be the cause of your good luck."

113

The New Origin of Good Luck

Since creating Good Luck
involves creating conditions . . .
Good Luck depends only on *you*.
Starting tomorrow,
you can also create Good Luck.

Sid bid farewell to Merlin with a firm and friendly embrace. He mounted his white horse and set off in search of adventure. Sid spent the rest of his days teaching other knights and non-knights, even children, the rules of Good Luck.

Now that he knew how to create Good Luck, he couldn't keep the secret to himself; Good Luck has to be shared.

The thing is, Sid found himself thinking: if he had been able to create so much Good Luck all by himself in only seven days, what might be if the entire Kingdom, if all its inhabitants, learned to create Good Luck for the rest of their lives?

Part Three

Finding Good Luck Again

Epilogue

After hearing the story, Jim took his shoes off too, and nestled his feet in the fresh clover that grew under the bench where the two friends were sitting.

Both remained silent, meditating about the story. Neither one of them said a thing. Almost two minutes went by. They were both thinking about something. Then, a tear ran down Jim's face. Max was the first to speak:

"I know what you're thinking, I'm sorry, Jim, I've made you feel uncomfortable—"

"Why?" asked Jim.

"I'm guessing that you think that was just a fable, a dumb story. I don't know. I didn't mean that you . . . I was only trying to help you have Good Luck."

"I was thinking precisely about that, Max. I was thinking how this story has come my way: meeting my childhood friend, whom I hadn't seen for fifty-four years, and telling me this story."

Max thought about it, about having met Jim so unexpectedly: truly a remarkable coincidence. It had been luck, not Good Luck. The Good Luck story had reached Jim by pure chance. How ironic! He told Jim:

"Yes, you're right. The story about Good Luck has reached you by chance."

"You think so?" Jim asked Max. "I was thinking just the opposite."

"Just the opposite?" asked Max, not knowing what Jim could possibly be referring to.

"Yes, just the opposite. I have been the one who has created the conditions to let this story reach me. To let Good Luck reach my hands."

"You?"

"Yes, Max. You and I have not met by chance. For the last four years, the worst in my life, my only hope was to find the only friend I ever had: you. During these last years, not a single day has gone by, that I didn't look for your face in all the people I came across. Each person that I bumped into, at every street light, every outdoor café, in every corner of the city. . . . I have never stopped scrutinizing each face, hoping to find yours. You are the only friend that I have and that I have ever had. Many times, I imagined I found you. I have often visualized how we would meet again, just as Sid visualized his clover growing. Sometimes, I even felt the hug we gave

121

each other just an hour ago. . . . I never stopped
thinking that this would happen."

Jim added:

"I have found you because I wanted to find you . . .
the Good Luck story has reached me, because I,
without knowing, was looking for it."

Visibly moved by this, Max told Jim:

"So you didn't think the story wasn't true. . . ."

"Correct," continued Jim, "I didn't think the story
wasn't true. Quite the contrary: our meeting has
proved to me that I can be like Sid, too. Today, I
have been the one who has created Good Luck. I can
create Good Luck, too. Do you realize that?"

"Of course I do," exclaimed Max.

And Jim asked Max, "Could I add one more rule to
your story?" And he said:

The Good Luck Story . . .

. . . never comes to you
by chance.

Max smiled at him. There was no need to say anything else. Words are often unnecessary between close friends. They hugged each other again. Max left, but Jim stayed, sitting on the bench resting his bare feet in the fresh clover that covered the grass of Central Park.

Jim felt something tickling his foot. He leaned forward and without looking, pulled something out of the ground. Something that brushed him very gently, something that seemed to want his attention.

It was a four-leaf clover.

Jim had decided, at his sixty-four years of age, to believe that he could create Good Luck.

How much longer are you going to wait?

Part Four

Some People Who Agree with Us

Ninety percent of success is based simply on insisting.
—Woody Allen

Conditions? What are conditions? I am the conditions!
—Napoleon Bonaparte

People are always blaming their circumstances for
what they are. I don't believe in circumstances. The
people who get on in this world are the people who get
up and look for the circumstances they want, and if
they can't find them, make them.
—George Bernard Shaw

Many people think that being talented is a great luck,
few, however, believe that luck can come with great talent.
—Jacinto Benavente

Luck only favors those minds ready for it.
—Isaac Asimov

Luck favors those with courage.
—Virgil

Luck is the excuse of those who fail.
—Pablo Neruda

The fruit of luck drops when it is ripe.
—Friedrich von Schiller

I strongly believe in luck and find out that the more I
work, the luckier I am.
—Stephen Leacock

The more I practice, the luckier I am.
—Gary Player

There's a door through which good luck enters, but you have the key.
—Japanese proverb

Our luck is not to be found outside us, but within us and in our willpower.
—Julius Grosse

Luck follows courage.
—Ennio

Of all those things that lead to luck, the safest ones are perseverance and work.
—Marie R. Reybaud

Luck helps those with courage.
—Publio Terencio

Whether inspiration comes, does not depend on me. The only thing that I can do is to make sure it finds me at work.
—Pablo Picasso

*Genius is 10 percent inspiration and 90 percent
perspiration.*
—Thomas Edison

*The secret to a great business consists in knowing
something that nobody else knows.*
—Aristotle Onassis

You are the cause of most things that happen to you.
—Nikki Lauda

*"And when do you plan to make your dream come
true?" the Master asked his disciple. "Whenever I
have the opportunity," he replied. But the Master
answered: "Opportunity never arrives, opportunity is
already here."*
—Anthony de Mello

God doesn't play dice with the Universe.
—Albert Einstein

Part Five

Decalogue, Moral of the Story, and New Origins of Good Luck

The Rules

First Rule of Good Luck

Luck doesn't last long, because it does not depend on you. Good Luck is created by each of us: that's why it lasts forever.

Second Rule of Good Luck

Many are those who want Good Luck, but few are those willing to pursue it.

Third Rule of Good Luck

If you have no Good Luck now, it might be because you're under the usual conditions. To have Good Luck, you must create new conditions.

Fourth Rule of Good Luck

Finding new conditions for Good Luck does not mean looking for our own benefit only. Creating conditions, helping others, makes Good Luck more likely to appear.

Fifth Rule of Good Luck

If you postpone the creation of new conditions, Good Luck never arrives. Creating new conditions is sometimes hard work, but . . . do it today!

Sixth Rule of Good Luck

Sometimes, even under the seemingly right conditions, Good Luck doesn't arrive. Look for the seemingly unnecessary but indispensable conditions in the small details.

Seventh Rule of Good Luck

To those who only believe in chance, creating conditions seems absurd. Those who create the conditions are not worried about chance.

Eighth Rule of Good Luck

Nobody can sell Good Luck. Good Luck cannot be sold. Do not trust those who sell luck.

Ninth Rule of Good Luck

After creating all the conditions, be patient, don't quit. For Good Luck to arrive, have faith.

Tenth Rule of Good Luck

Creating Good Luck consists in preparing conditions for opportunity. But opportunity has nothing to do with luck or chance: it is always there.

Moral of the Story

Creating Good Luck consists only in . . . creating the conditions.

The New Origin of Good Luck

Since creating Good Luck involves creating conditions . . . Good Luck depends only on *you*. Starting tomorrow, *you* can also create Good Luck.

The Good Luck Story . . .

. . . never comes to you by chance.

Postscript

This book was written in eight hours, straight through.

However, it took us over three years to create it.

Some people will only remember the eight hours.

Others will only remember the three years.

The first ones will believe we were just lucky.

The others will believe that we created the conditions for Good Luck.

Acknowledgments

To Gregorio Vlastelica, our editor at Urano,
who believed in this project from the very
beginning. Thanks to his sensibility and generosity
this story has a wider reach than the authors could
have expected.

To Isabel Monteagudo and Maru de Montserrat,
our literary agents, for their eagerness and strength.
For the hundreds of hours spent contacting
publishers all over the world and for getting a fable
by two guys from Barcelona to see the light
simultaneously in so many places; certainly, a rare
publishing event.

To all International Editors' coagents and
especially to Laura Dail for her tenacity and faith
in this little book. Only she could see that *Good Luck*
would be published throughout the English-
speaking world.

To Susan R. Williams, our editor in the United States
and in the rest of the English-speaking world. Susan
had the courage to bet on this book and make of it
an international project.

To Philip Kotler, for his wonderful quote,
which he allowed us to use in all editions and
languages, and for his priceless help in making
sure the book would be published in the United
States.

To Emilio Mayo, with whom we've shared Good
Luck for seven years now and hope to continue to
share for many more.

To Jordi Nadal, our own personal Merlin, for his
talent and friendship.

To Manel Armengol, a true Sid, friend, and mate. He gave us the strength to set off in search of clovers.

To Josep López, because his publishing experience is an endless source of inspiration and improvement.

To Josep Feliu, for his illustrations that inspired each and every character in the story.

To Jorge Escribano, for showing us the path to the Enchanted Forest and how to create the conditions for a *Clover* to grow.

To Adolfo Blanco, whose brilliant comments and contributions to the first draft helped us see the positive things in it.

To Montse Serret for his help and passion since she read the first manuscript.

To all our colleagues at ESADE, and to all the participants in our seminars and courses, for being a source of inspiration and imagination.

To María, Blanca, and Alejo for their support and for the many hours stolen. They are behind this story, in every sentence, in every word.

To Mónica, Laia, and Pol for their love and affection. You are the reason it makes sense every day to create the conditions that let *Magic Clovers* grow.

The Authors

Alex Rovira heads the qualitative division of marketing consulting firm Salvetti & Llombart. His previous experience includes marketing positions with several companies and the founding of his own consultancy. He is also a well-known speaker in the field of psychology. He is author of *The Inner Compass* (Urano, 2004) and the Spanish-language edition of *Understanding the Consumer* (with Bernard Dubois, Prentice Hall, 1998).

Fernando Trías de Bes cofounded and directs Salvetti & Llombart. He has held marketing positions with several multinationals. He is coauthor (with Philip Kotler) of *Lateral Marketing* (Wiley, 2003).

The authors have worked with many top organizations through Salvetti & Llombart, including Bayer, Credit-Suisse, Dannon, Frito-Lay, Hewlett-Packard, Mercedes-Benz, Microsoft, Morgan Stanley, Nestlé, Oxfam, Paramount, PepsiCo, Sony, and Universal. They have also collaborated with consultancies such as McKinsey & Co., AT Kearney, and Bain & Company.

Both are professors of marketing at ESADE Business School (Barcelona, Spain), one Europe's most respected business schools; Rovira also teaches courses in human resources.